18 Special Worship Celebrations

Worship Services
For Congregational Use

Cynthia E. Cowen

D0066743

CSS Publishing Company, Inc.
Lima, Ohio

Second Printing 1995

Copyright © 1994 by
The CSS Publishing Company, Inc.
Lima, Ohio

Library of Congress Cataloging-in-Publication Data

Cowen, Cynthia E., 1947-
    18 special worship celebrations : worship services for congregational use / by Cynthia E. Cowen
        p.   cm.
    ISBN1-55673-830-7
    1. Worship programs. 2. Occasional services. I. Title. II. Title: Eighteen special worship celebrations.
BV198.C88   1994
264—dc20   93-37990
                                                                                 CIP

ISBN 1-55673-830-7   PRINTED IN U.S.A.

This resource is dedicated to the women of the Northern Great Lakes Synod who have given me so many wonderful opportunities to create for them and to the Synodical Women's Organization Board of the Women of the Evangelical Lutheran Church in America who for five years encouraged and allowed me to develop programs and worship services for special events. The love and affirmation of this community and the greater body of Christ, the church, has been a real blessing to me in my writing.

Table Of Contents

 Summary

Worship 1 — A Celebration Of Worship
Opening To A Special Meeting
Theme: Celebrating the Creator God
  This service is designed for worship or an opening to a special meeting. It includes Celebrating The Creator (call to worship, hymn, prayer of the day), Celebrating The Word (lesson, responsive psalm, anthem, gospel, place for sermon, hymn), Celebrating Our Offerings (offering and announcements), Litany Of Celebration (spells out CELEBRATE and is read responsively), Celebrating Through Prayer (prayers of the church and Lord's Prayer) and Celebrating God's Constant Presence (closing remarks, benediction, hymn).

Worship 2 — Believing We Belong
Celebration Service Of Holy Communion
Theme: Belief in God, which joins us together in community
  This celebration of communion is for use in worship or a large assembly or convention. We Believe We Belong To A Merciful God (invocation, confession, hymn), We Praise The God To Whom We Belong (litany of praise, prayer of the day), We Believe In God's Holy Word (lessons, anthem, gospel, meditation, hymn), We Confess Our Belief (creed), We Belong To God In Community (prayers, sharing of the peace, offering), We Belong To A God Who Died For Us (service of communion, Lord's Prayer), Believing We Go Forth (benediction and hymn).

Worship 3 — Evening Vesper Service
Closing Night Worship
Theme: Entering God's presence at the close of day
  This is a closing night worship service. We Belong In God's Presence (invocation and hymn), We Believe In The Word (litany based on Psalm 42:1-8), We Belong To A Merciful God (prayer and hymn), We Believe In A God Who Speaks (place for evening meditation, reflection and offering), We Belong To A God Who Hears And Answers (prayers of community, Lord's Prayer, benediction and hymn).

Worship 4 — How Blessed To Work In Unity
Morning Devotional Service
Theme: Unity in a light and enlightening devotional worship
  This is a morning devotional service. The resource opens with an invocation and hymn, uses a litany of unity, calls the body to be united in faith and prayer, scripture, meditations, reflection and hymns to show how to be united in purpose, action and community. It concludes with a

Blessedness Of Unity (remarks, Psalm 133 and hymn). Three meditations accompany this service. Each brings humor to the service. Meditation 1, "Vegetate or Cultivate?" has vegetables discussing the plight of the farmer. Meditation 2, "Sour Grapes or Sweet Wine?" examines fruit of the vineyard. Meditation 3, "A Great Chili!" challenges all to plunge into their work by adding their gifts to enhance the flavor of the brew.

Worship 5 — Love, Love, Love — That's What It's All About
Youth Service For Mother's Day
Theme: Love shown by God and by us to others, especially our mothers
     This service includes an order of worship for a Sunday morning service. It has a litany, prayer of the day, music, lessons, hymns, confession of sin, prayers and closing litany. Special music is "Love, Love, Love," by Herbert Brokering, Augsburg/Fortress, 1970.

Worship 6 — God's Shining Lights
Sunday Morning Holy Communion
Theme: Lights shining in a dark world
     This service is a communion service during Sunday morning worship. It opens with a call to worship and hymn, and The Light Grows Into A Litany Of Light (children's choir, lessons, places for children's message and sermon, hymn and offering). It moves to a confession (Confession Of Darkness And Light), and absolution and creed, God's Light Revealed (communion), Recognizing Special Lights (honoring Sunday school teachers — present candles for each teacher). It includes prayers of the church, benediction and closing hymn.

Worship 7 — Litany Of Freedom
Memorial Day Observance
Theme: Freedom
     This is a Memorial Day observance. It may be used as an addition to a regular order of service by the congregation on this day. Introductory comments by the leader may be omitted.

Worship 8 — Behold The Glory Of The Lord!
Nursing Home Service With Holy Communion
Theme: God's glory
     This is a service for use in nursing homes or regular worship with communion. It includes an invocation, hymns, Litany Of God's Glory Acclaimed, prayer of the day, The Word Reveals God's Glory (lessons and place for meditation), Jesus Reveals His Glory (confession and absolution), celebration of communion, Lord's Prayer and benediction.

Worship 9 — Healing Of Divisions
Prayer Service
Theme: Healing the divisions of the world, nation and congregation
     This is a prayer service. It uses hymns, readings and special remarks, which call God's people to adoration, praise, confession and intercession.

Prayers and readings are included for justice, all people, end to prejudice, unity, nation and government and the congregation. The service ends with the Lord's Prayer, benediction and hymn.

Worship 10 — A Celebration Of Baptism
Baptism Worship Service
Theme: Birthday Celebration

This is a service of worship. It is ideal for summer picnic fellowship and worship. Bulletins may include hymns and order of service. The service assists the congregation to enlarge and enhance baptism in the faith and life of its members. A baptismal message prepares participants to affirm their baptism at the close of the service. A place for prayers of the church, Lord's Prayer and a benediction concludes the service.

Worship 11 — A Galilean Service
Lakeside Service With Holy Communion
Theme: Outdoor ministry of Christ around the Sea of Galilee

This is appropriate as a lakeside service with communion. It includes, The Scene Is Set (responsive reading from Matthew 4), opening hymn, Christ's Ministry To Those Around The Lake (responsive reading from Mark 6), hymn of praise, The Word Ministers To Us (Psalm 42, lessons, place for sermon, hymn), We Respond To The Word (creed, prayers, offering, prayer), The Lord Feeds Us With His Presence and Christ Feeds us (communion service, Lord's Prayer, hymns), and Our Response Of Love (responsive reading from John 21), benediction and closing hymn.

Worship 12 — Showers Of Blessing
Worship Service With A Skit
Theme: Blessings throughout the service using a skit

This is a worship service with a skit. It is ideal for women's meetings. It uses hymns, confession, Apostles' Creed, scripture readings and a skit titled "Come Under God's Umbrella." The props (umbrellas) spell JESUS. Hymns may be inserted on the bulletins.

Worship 13 — Blessing Through Marriage
Marriage Anniversary Service
Theme: Marriage

This is a service to commemorate wedding anniversaries. It may be used to celebrate the anniversary of a couple within the congregation. Hymns, scripture, reflection, prayers and blessing make a special recognition of the anniversary of marriage.

Worship 14 — The Blessing Of Giving
Post-Lenten Ingathering Service
Theme: Giving to the Lord

This is a post-Lenten ingathering service insert. This insert may be used to collect an offering of a Lenten tithe. A reflection of giving, a reading, an opportunity to come forward and present the offering, and prayer follow the theme of giving.

Worship 15 — A Feast Of Worship
Following Soup And Sandwich Supper
Theme: God prepares a feast for us

This is a special worship service ideal to use following a soup and sandwich supper during Lent or Advent, council retreat or lock-in. We Prepare Our Hearts (preparation for worship), We Examine The Kettle (examination of heart), Cleaning The Pot (confession and absolution), We Praise The Cook (Litany of praise based on Psalm 34), Listen To The Recipe (lessons), Add The Ingredients (place for meditations), Simmer Until Done (prayers of community, Lord's Prayer, benediction and closing hymn). The children's story, *Stone Soup*, with a reflection of the lessons is ideal for this service.

Worship 16 — A Dedication Of Hand Chimes
Dedication Of Gift In Memorial
Theme: Music

This is an insert for the dedication of a gift in memorial. It includes a responsive litany of praise and presentation and concludes with a prayer of dedication.

Worship 17 — Installation Of Pastor
Receiving A New Leader
Theme: Celebrate reception of a new leader

A special service to install a pastor or other ordained leader of the congregation. A regular order of worship (processional hymn, invocation, scripture, anthem, and place for meditation) comes before the installation service. The Service Of Installation is conducted by an installing presider (remarks, creed). Representatives of the church present the pastor for installation (readings and remarks on the pastoral ministry). Also included is a pastor's response and congregational responses, God Hears And Answers Prayers (installed pastor conducts the prayers of the church and Lord's Prayer). Service ends with benediction and recessional hymn.

Worship 18 — For All The Saints
For All Saints' Day
Theme: Remembering saints of the church

A service for All Saints' Day. A regular order of service includes a special call to worship, a responsive confessional litany, an absolution, a litany of mercy, and a place for the regular prayer of the day, anthem, hymns, readings, sermon, creed, offering, petitions of prayer, Lord's Prayer and benediction. Special music by John Yivisaker, "I Was There To Hear Your Borning Cry," 1985 may be used.

1

A Celebration Of Worship

Opening To A Special Meeting

We Celebrate The Creator

Call To Worship

L: We call upon you, O God of Creation, who spoke the Word and created the heavens and earth, who said, "Let there be light," and there was light, who separated the light from the darkness.

C: Be present in our celebration of worship.

L: We call upon you, O Jesus Christ, through whom all things were made, in whom there is life which is the light of humankind, and from whom light shines into the darkness of our souls.

11

C: Be present in our celebration of worship.

L: We call upon you, O Holy Spirit, who hovering over the waters at creation moves mightily in our lives. Stir up the waters of our baptism and allow the light to shine into our hearts.

C: Be present in our celebration of worship.

L: Come, Triune God, be present as we celebrate your place in our lives and in all of creation.

C: Amen. Come, O God of creation.

Opening Hymn Of Celebration

Prayer Of The Day:

L: Join our hearts in celebration now, Almighty God. Bless our worship as we come together seeking your divine presence in our lives and the life of your church. Stir us creatively that we may join others throughout the world who celebrate your love. Guide us daily planting your vision within our hearts. In Jesus' name,

C: Amen.

We Celebrate The Word Proclaimed

First Reading

Second Reading

Psalm 150

L: Praise the Lord! Praise God in his sanctuary;

C: Praise him in his mighty firmament!

L: Praise him for his mighty deeds;

C: **Praise him according to his surpassing greatness!**

L: Praise him with trumpet sound;

C: **Praise him with lute and harp!**

L: Praise him with tambourine and dance;

C: **Praise him with strings and pipe!**

L: Praise him with clanging cymbals;

C: **Praise him with loud clashing cymbals!**

L: Let everything that breathes praise the Lord!

C: **Praise the Lord!**

Anthem

The Proclamation Of The Gospel:
L: A Reading from the Holy Gospel

C: **Open our ears to hear, O Lord!**

Gospel Lesson
L: The Gospel of the Lord!

C: **Open our hearts to understand, O Lord!**

Sermon

Hymn Of Celebration

We Celebrate Our Offerings

Announcements

Offerings

Special Music

Offertory

Litany Of Celebration

We stand and praise the creator God:

C - L: CHRIST, Jesus, we CELEBRATE our CARING love and CREATIVE energy.

    C: We praise the God of Creation.

E - L: EVERLASTING God, we celebrate your ENTRY into ETERNAL life through Jesus Christ your son.

    C: We praise the God of Salvation.

L - L: LIVING LORD, we LONG to LIFT up praise with our LIPS in LANGUAGES which celebrate your gracious LOVE.

    C: We praise the God of Love.

E - L: ELOHIM, God of our Fathers, we ENTER your presence EAGERLY anticipating your ENTRY into our world again.

    C: We praise the God of Revelation.

B - L: BRIGHT Morning Star, we BRING BEFORE you our BROKENNESS asking you to BIND our wounds and to heal us through your BODY and BLOOD.

C: We praise the God of Wholeness.

R - L: ROD of Jesse, we RECOGNIZE that our RIGHT-EOUSNESS is as filthy RAGS.

C: We praise the God of Redemption.

A - L: ALMIGHTY God, we stand in AWE of your ACTION in our lives and in ALL creation.

C: We praise the God of Power and Might.

T - L: TRUE God and TRUE Light, we TRUST in you TO TURN our TIME and efforts into works which TRULY glorify THY name.

C: We praise the God of Truth.

E - L: ETERNAL Word, continue your creative work in EACH of us until EVERY creature stands redeemed and ENTERS their ETERNAL rest.

C: We praise the God of Sanctification.

We Celebrate Through Prayer

L: As we celebrate God, our great Creator, we acknowledge that he desires to give us, his precious children, all good things. Hear us now, All Loving Father, as we offer our prayers and thanksgiving before your throne, through Jesus Christ our Lord.

C: Hear our prayers, Almighty God.

15

Prayers of The Church

L: Lord, in your mercy,

C: **Hear our prayer.**

L: Almighty God, has heard our prayers and according to his perfect will has bestowed his answer. In that confidence we pray the prayer our Lord taught us to pray:

Lord's Prayer

We Celebrate God's Constant Presence

L: As we have gathered as a caring community united in Christ Jesus our Lord, may we continue to grow in faith as we leave God's sanctuary now. May we affirm each other in our homes, community, and work place. May we support each other in our individual callings. May we continue to minister under the power of the Spirit in acts of loving service. May we be made well and whole so that we can share the good news in God's church, our society, and the world. May our lives be a constant witness to the celebration of the life of Christ to all around us.

C: **We celebrate God's constant presence. Amen.**

Benediction:

L: The blessing of the Creator God, the Son through whom all things were created, and the Spirit who moves in our hearts and throughout all creation, be with us now as we go forth renewed and committed to Jesus Christ our Lord of all creation. Go in peace, serve the Lord.

C: **Thanks be to God!**

Closing Hymn Of Celebration

2

Believing We Belong

A Celebration Service
Of Holy Communion

We Believe We Belong To A Merciful God

Invocation:

Holy Spirit, we call upon you to fill us now with the spirit of worship. Creator God, send forth your love enabling us to totally offer to you our lives poured out in true spiritual worship. Remembering the sacrifice of your dear Son, Jesus Christ, we acknowledge that we belong to you, Almighty God. Fill us with the faith we need to exercise that belief as we praise your wonderful name.

C: Come, Holy Spirit.

Confession:

L: Gracious God, you look upon us in love knowing that we often stray from your perfect path. Our wills guide us to be self-serving. Our desires are not always pure. Our spirits

17

are not always in tune with your voice. However, we know that when we sin, we have one who stands before you and pleads for us, Jesus Christ. Through him, we have access to your throne of grace. Hear our confessions and be merciful to us, your wayward children.

C: **Most Merciful Father, we acknowledge that we are sinners in need of a Savior. Our thoughts, our words, our actions at times are not right. We often say and do things for which we are ashamed. We neglect to take time for you in our busy schedules. We miss opportunities to share Christ's love with family and friends. We ignore the needs of those around us. We become dissatisfied with our lives and often murmur not recognizing our many blessings. Looking to the world, we at times become envious of what we see our neighbor has and complain about what we don't have. Forgive us, Gracious God, and cleanse us now through the precious blood of our Lord and Savior, Jesus Christ. Renew and strengthen us in your mercy, that we may be lights to a darkened world. Center our wills and desires on Christ through whom we pray. Amen.**

L: The Father looks upon us in mercy through Jesus Christ his Son. For his sake, Almighty God, forgive our sins. Believing in Jesus Christ, we are given the power to become children of God and are blessed with the Holy Spirit.

C: **Amen.**

Opening Hymn

We Praise The God To Whom We Belong

L: The grace of our Lord Jesus Christ in whom we believe, the love of the Father to whom we belong, and the fellowship of the Holy Spirit be with you all.

C: **And also with you.**

Litany Of Praise

L: Almighty God, we come together as a community united in Jesus the Christ,

C: **And we praise your name forever.**

L: We honor the Prince of Peace and the Rock of our salvation,

C: **And we praise your name forever.**

L: We pray for peace on earth and for wholeness in the body of Christ, his beloved Church,

C: **And we praise your name forever.**

L: We come today to offer our worship,

C: **And we praise your name forever.**

L: We thank you, O Blessed Savior, for your body and blood shared in communion,

C: **And we praise your name forever.**

L: We ask your divine help, your loving comfort, and your mighty protection,

C: **And we praise your name forever.**

L: We rejoice in the victory of our Lord over sin and death,

C: **And we praise your name forever.**

L: We offer to you, O God, the honor and glory due your name,

C: **And we praise your name forever.**

L: We believe we belong to a mighty and gracious God,

C: And we praise that name forever. Alleluia, Alleluia. Amen.

Prayer Of The Day

L: The Lord be with you.

C: And also with you.

L: Let us pray:
Loving Father, you created us in your image and called us
to live in community with each other and in harmony with
your perfect will. Look with favor upon us as we endeavor
to be true disciples of Jesus Christ our Lord. Empower us
as we commit ourselves to grow in faith. Stir up your gifts
within us that we may support each other in the calling you
have placed upon our lives. Help us to serve you in the many
areas of ministry and action you provide. And bring healing and wholeness to your creation, and to the church, the
society, and the world.

C: Amen.

We Believe In God's Holy Word

First Lesson

Anthem

Second Lesson

Alleluia Verse

Announcement Of The Gospel

Gospel Chant: "Glory to you, O Lord."

Gospel

Gospel Chant: "Praise to you, O Christ."

Meditation

Hymn

We Confess Our Belief

L: Having heard the Word proclaimed, we respond in belief in Christ Jesus our Lord, and confess the faith of the church, the faith we hold in the one to whom we belong.

L: Do you believe in God, the Creator?

C: **I believe in God, the Father Almighty, Creator of heaven and earth.**

I believe that I am created in the image of the God to whom I belong.

L: Do you believe in Jesus Christ?

C: **I believe in Jesus Christ, his only Son, our Lord. He was conceived by the power of the Holy Spirit and born of the Virgin Mary. He suffered under Pontius Pilate, was crucified, died, and was buried. He descended into hell. On the third day he rose again. He ascended into heaven, and is seated at the right hand of the Father. He will come again to judge the living and the dead.**

I believe that I am called to be a disciple of Jesus Christ to whom I belong.

L: Do you believe in the Holy Spirit?

C: I believe in the Holy Spirit, the Holy Catholic Church, the communion of saints, the forgiveness of sins, the resurrection of the body, and the life everlasting.

I believe that I am empowered by the Holy Spirit to whom I belong.

We Belong To God In Community

Prayers

L: Lord, in your mercy,

C: Hear our prayer.

L: The peace of the Lord be with you always.

C: And also with you.

Sharing Of The Peace

Offering

Offertory

We Belong To A God Who Died For Us

L: The Lord be with you.

C: And also with you.

L: As we lift up our hearts,

C: We acknowledge the God who died for us.

L: As we give thanks to the Lord our God,

C: **We thank and praise him for his sacrifice.**

L: It is right that we should offer thanks and praise to you, Creator God, through Christ Jesus our Lord, who comes to harvest the souls of the seeds that have been sown through faith by the Spirit. The earth blossoms, the harvest ripens, and all of humankind rejoices as the Lord reaps the bounty. Therefore, we join as your church on earth with the hosts of heaven in praising your holy name.

C: **Holy, holy, holy Lord, God of pow'r and might: heaven and earth are full of your glory, hosanna, hosanna, hosanna, in the highest. Blessed is he who comes in the name of the Lord. Hosanna in the highest.**

Words Of Institution:

L: In the night in which our Lord Jesus was betrayed, he took bread, and gave thanks; broke it, and gave it to his disciples, saying Take, eat for this is my body, given for you. Do this in remembrance of me.

After supper, he took the cup, offered thanks, and gave it to all to drink, saying: This cup is the new covenant in my blood, shed for you and for all people for the forgiveness of sin. Do this in remembrance of me.

As often as we eat this bread and drink of this cup, we are proclaiming our Lord's death until he comes again.

C: **Christ has died. Christ has risen. Christ will come again!**

L: Send now your Holy Spirit that all who share in this bread and cup may be reconciled to you, Almighty Lord, through belief in your Son, Jesus Christ, and his sacrifice for them.

C: **Amen. Come, Holy Spirit.**

L: Join our prayers with your servants of every time and place, uniting them with the ceaseless petitions of Jesus, our great high priest, until he comes for the final harvest.

C: **Through the God who loved us, the God who died for us, and the God who rose again, we, who are united in the Holy Spirit, give honor and glory to you, Almighty Father, now and forever. Amen.**

Lord's Prayer

Distribution Of Communion

Communion Hymns

L: Our Lord's body and blood strengthen you and keep you in his grace.

C: **Amen.**

L: Let us pray. Pour out your spirit upon this community which you have fed and united with your body and blood; through Jesus Christ our Lord.

C: **Amen.**

Believing We Go Forth

Benediction

L: May the blessing of the God to whom we know we belong go with us, encouraging us to daily walk and profess the faith in which we believe. May you become all that God has called you to as disciples of Christ Jesus the Lord and may you be a blessing to God and to those you touch. In the name of the Father who created you, and of the Son who has died for you, and the Holy Spirit who sanctifies you.

C: **Amen**

Closing Hymn

3

Evening Vesper Service

Closing Night Service

We Belong In God's Presence

Invocation:

L: We call upon the Lord to be present with us now at the close of our day. We turn to face the Creator, to whom we all belong, offering our songs of praise. Give ear, Almighty Lord, as we enter your presence through Jesus Christ your Son. Holy Spirit, rest upon us in peace quieting our souls. Whisper to us of your love as we breathe in the sweetness of your everlasting presence.

C: Come, Holy Spirit. Amen.

Opening Hymn: "Abide With Me"

We Believe In The Word

Litany
(Based on Psalm 42:1-8)

L: As the deer pants for streams of water,

C: Lord, I pant for thee.

L: As the soul thirsts for God Almighty,

C: Lord, I thirst for thee.

L: Tears have been my food day and night,

C: Lord, wipe away my tears.

L: I pour out my soul unto you,

C: Lord, incline your ear to hear.

L: O, soul, why are you so downcast within me?

C: Lord, lift up mine eyes.

L: O, soul, be not disturbed,

C: Lord, my trust and hope rest in you.

L: Deep calls to deep in the roar of your waterfalls.

C: Lord, deep calls to deep in the spirit.

L: By day you direct my paths in love,

C: Lord, at night your song is with me.

L: I enter your house with thanksgiving,

C: Lord, hear my prayer of worship.

We Belong To A Merciful God

Prayer

L: Almighty God, we come to you at the close of this day reflecting on all that has occurred. Forgive us our failures at not being faithful to your call. Forgive us for missed opportunities to share your love with others. Forgive us for time spent apart from you. Cleanse us, now, Merciful Lord, through the precious blood of your Son, so that our spirits may rest in peace. In Christ, we pray.

C: Amen.

Hymn Of Meditation: "Now The Day Is Over"

We Believe In A God Who Speaks

Evening Meditation STUDY/DISCUSSION of REVELATION

Silent Reflection And Receiving Of The Offering

 HYMN

We Belong To A God Who Hears And Answers

Prayers

L: Lord God, we come to you now with the prayers of our hearts. Hear us as we offer up our concerns to the throne of grace that your will be done perfectly in each situation. Lord in your mercy,

C: Hear our prayer.

(Prayers of the community are lifted.)

27

L: We entrust these prayers to your heavenly care through Jesus Christ our Lord, and close with the prayer our Lord taught us to pray:

The Lord's Prayer

Benediction:

L: Having offered up our worship and praise, we now ask God's blessing upon us as we rest in the shelter of his everlasting wings. May the Lord bless and keep us, make his face to shine upon us and be gracious unto us. May the Lord look upon each of us with favor, and give us peace. In the name of the Father, the Son, and the Holy Spirit.

C: Amen.

Closing Hymn: "All Praise To Thee"

4

How Blessed To Work In Unity

Morning Devotional Service

Invocation:

L: As morning has broken, break now, O God, into our midst. May this day bring glory to your name and to your work among us.

C: **Bless us with your presence, Almighty God.**

Hymn: "Lord, Whose Love In Humble Service"

Litany Of Unity

L: God created the heavens and the earth,

C: **Creator God, renew us this day.**

L: God cleanses the heart and plants purpose within,

C: **Holy Spirit, create in us clean hearts united in mission.**

L: Jesus was in the Father, and the Father in him,

C: Be in our hearts and day, Lord Jesus.

L: God desires that we live in harmony with him and with one another,

C: Heavenly Father, unite us in spirit through Christ Jesus our Lord. Amen.

United In Faith

L: As there is one body and one Spirit, God calls us to be one acknowledging one Lord, one faith, one baptism, one God and Father of all, who is above all and through all and in all.

Apostles' Creed *(All)*:

I believe in God, the Father Almighty, Creator of heaven and earth.

I believe in Jesus Christ, his only Son, our Lord. He was conceived by the power of the Holy Spirit and born of the Virgin Mary. He suffered under Pontius Pilate, was crucified, died, and was buried. He descended into hell. On the third day he rose again. He ascended into heaven, and is seated at the right hand of the Father. He will come again to judge the living and the dead.

I believe in the Holy Spirit, the Holy Catholic Church, the communion of saints, the forgiveness of sins, the resurrection of the body, and the life everlasting. Amen.

United in Prayer

L: As we have confessed our unity in faith, let us pray the prayer that binds us together and unites us with God.

Lord's Prayer *(All:)*

Our Father who art in heaven, hallowed be your name. Your kingdom come, your will be done, on earth as in heaven.

Give us today our daily bread. Forgive us our sins as we forgive those who sin against us. Save us from the time of trial and deliver us from evil. For the kingdom, the power, and the glory are yours, now and forever. Amen.

United In Purpose

First Reading: Romans 12:3-8

Meditation: "Vegetate Or Cultivate?"

Silence For Reflection

Hymn: "Take My Life, That I May Be" (vv. 1 & 2)

United In Action

Second Reading: 2 Corinthians 1:3-7

Meditation: "Sour Grapes Or Sweet Wine?"

Silence For Reflection

Hymn: "Take My Life, That I May Be" (vv. 3 & 4)

United in Community

Third Reading: Ephesians 4:11-16

Meditation: "A Great Chili!"

Silence For Reflection

Hymn: "Take My Life, That I May Be" (vv. 5 & 6)

The Blessedness Of Unity

L: As we have reflected on our purpose for being here, and considered our individual actions, and yielded to working in community with God and one another, let us now declare the blessedness that unity will give us.

Psalm 133

L: How very good and pleasant it is when kindred live together in unity!

C: **It is like the precious oil on the head,**

L: Running down upon the beard, on the beard of Aaron,

C: **Running down over the collar of his robes.**

L: It is like the dew of Hermon,

C: **Which falls on the mountains of Zion.**

L: For there the Lord ordained his blessing,

C: **Life evermore. Amen.**

Sent Forth United

Benediction:
L: Go forth into this day, united in heart and purpose, through Jesus Christ our Lord.

C: **Send us forth obedient to your will, Almighty God. Amen.**

Hymn: "We Plow The Fields And Scatter"

Vegetate Or Cultivate?

Meditation 1

Reading: Romans 12:3-8

The plight of the farmer had drawn all the vegetables together in the root cellar of his home for the first time in the annals of their history. "I've called you all here tonight," announced the ACORN SQUASH, "to SQUASH these rumors that there is a STRAIN on our community."

"But there is!" the ONION PEALED out. "I could just CRY when I think of our farmer's economic plight. TEARS brim up from under my THIN SKIN."

"I'm BOILING mad and could MASH all of you," the POTATO sputtered. "Look at my red EYES. I'm tired of trying to SPROUT solutions on my own."

"Well, I thought I could certainly TURN UP an answer to this PICKLE he's in," replied the TURNIP.

"BEATS me what all this fussing's about. My GREENS added color to his dull meal tonight," the BEET pridefully BLUSHED.

"SHUCKS, I've been all EARS listening to each of you sputter about this dilemma tonight," drawled the EAR of CORN. "Let me share some KERNELS of advice."

The corn's silky hair and erect stalk gave him a certain amount of credibility among the rows of vegetables assembled. "We've all been doing our own thing, not taking into consideration the hard labor and love the farmer puts in. He carefully plants, cultivates, waters, weeds out that which might harm us, and then harvests us when we are ripe for picking. We're all in this garden together, so let's cooperate in the only way we know how now to make our task profitable. As we combine our efforts at growing, we will produce a bumper crop this season. In the mean time, we can arrange to come together and produce delicious meals for his table each day. If we just stop vegetating and looking to our own special interests, we will start to really produce for the one who truly cares for us. Certainly, for all he has done, uniting together is not a difficult response."

They all agreed that night to take the corn's advice, and though the farmer did not become wealthy that first year, through continued effort in time his harvest became more plentiful.

Jesus calls us to set aside our differences and unite to further his kingdom here on earth. God has carefully planted the life of Christ in us, cultivated the life of faith with his Word, watered it in his love, and weeded out sin which would choke out our very existence. Our response, as we work in unity with one another, will yield great harvests.

Jesus stated that unless a kernel of wheat falls to the ground and dies, it remains only a seed. He died that we might have abundant life. As we die to self and our own agendas we become part of a team working for a common purpose — to share the good news. Join those who labor at planting, those who till the soil, and those who are blessed to harvest his crops. As we work, let us cease just vegetating and be cultivators of our corners of the garden so as to yield bumper crops for Jesus this year.

Sour Grapes Or Sweet Wine?
Meditation 2

Reading: 2 Corinthians 1:3-7

Hanging around the vineyard one bright, sunny day, a variety of grape bunches held a discussion on the prospect of their futures.

"There are many options open to each of us," began one plump, red grape. "I plan on offering my juices for quenching the thirst of many."

"Well, I don't relish having MY juices squeezed out that way," a modest, young, green grape replied. "It's much too painful. I'd rather expose myself to the sun and become a raisin."

"Bother, bother, bother ..." chimed in a bunch of immature clusters hanging around the fringe of the arbor. "We don't plan on contributing anything to this vineyard. We've decided to sink our roots into different soil. When the vinedresser takes one bite of our fruit, he'll know that our sourness won't be of much good. We'll show him that we're not to be shoved around. What about you?'' they asked turning to the best grape bunch in the vineyard.

Slowly and deliberately, these mature grapes replied, ''What a privilege it has been to have our soil toiled and fertilized. The sun and rain have done their best to ripen us so we could produce the best for the Caretaker. So, we'll choose to offer ourselves up to the winepress.''

''But the pain involved in being squeezed out like that!'' the little raisins whined. ''And the length of time you have to just sit around and ferment. It takes longer to become wine than juice. Besides that, you lose your identity. Why would you choose that?''

''The Caretaker wants us to be all we can be, the best. How else do we respond but by willingly giving up ourselves to be just that.''

How like this group we might become. Some might be willing to become grape juice. We don't mind a little pain and suffering in our lives. In fact, we might even see it as a badge of service. But to have discomfort prolonged is more than many of us can bear. Some don't want to be squeezed out, so prefer to become dried up. Cut off from the vine, Christ, we shrivel. However, unlike a raisin which is edible after the drying process, we wither, decay, and are not palatable or of use to anyone. Sour grapes people have deliberately chosen to be disobedient to their Caretaker. They refuse to add any of their talents to the productivity of the vineyard. Yet those who choose to become that special, sweet wine are willing to suffer — to give up time and comforts — to give up their interests for the interest of God — in order that they might help others bringing them comfort and encouragement — affirming and uplifting. They know that the love and care of God is so special that they are willing to endure for as long as it takes to have their juices become that tasteful wine for others to drink of.

Go the extra step in your work. Don't dry up, cutting yourself off from interacting. Don't just become juice, adding a little to the brew. Don't alienate yourselves and be sour grapes. Let your creative juices overflow and pour out for each other.

35

A Great Chili!
Meditation 3

Reading: Ephesians 4:11-16

A tomato refused to allow the cook to add it to the already bubbling brew in the kettle. "You've got to be kidding! Why should I add my plump, luscious body to that conglomeration? Just look at it: hamburger, onions, sauce, kidney beans, AND potatoes! Whoever heard of potatoes in chili!"

"But your unique characteristics will add so much to this special meal," the onion cried out. "Your pulp and juice will blend nicely giving our soup special flavor."

"Reconsider joining us," the ingredients churned in unison. "We promise not to cover you up."

"Well, maybe it's worth the sacrifice. I do care for the cook who nurtured me in her garden and watered me during that drought. This plunge could add a new dimension to my life. Okay — move over — here I come!"

What a gift we bring today as we gather to work with each other in mission. Our unique talents added with others' gifts enhance the purpose of the church. As we pool our insights and gifting with others, new works can be created and others sustained. God is the chef in our kitchen bringing us together so that we can learn from each other. Experience, knowledge, enthusiasm, vision, and so much more all come together for the benefit of the body. Plunge into your day, plunge into your special brew, and allow the Spirit to stir you. Even if the recipe might look strange, let God do the concocting. He knows just which ingredients to add to bring about just the right flavor. Make your great chilis or whatever else the Great Chef decides to create in and through this day.

36

5

Love, Love, Love — That's What It's All About

Youth Service For Mother's Day

Call To Worship:

L: We call upon the God of love to be present in our worship. Let us open our hearts to receive his love. Let us respond to that love with our praise and adoration.

C: **We give to our loving Lord the blessing and honor he deserves. Amen.**

Opening Hymn: "Blessing And Honor"

Showered With Love

L: The Lord reigns on high;

C: **And showers us with love.**

L: The Lamb of God, who offered himself up as a sacrifice for our sin and rose from the dead, lives within our hearts;

C: **And showers us with love.**

L: The Spirit is poured out on all who open their hearts and lives to receive Jesus as Lord and Savior;

C: **And showers us with love.**

Prayer Of The Day

L: Pour out upon us now, Gracious Spirit, the love of God found in Christ Jesus our Lord. Stir us to respond to others with a deeper love and understanding. May our hearts overflow with loving gratitude for your love shown to us this day.

C: **Amen.**

Special Music By Youth Choirs

First Lesson

Second Lesson

Gospel Announced
C: **Glory to you, O Lord.**

Gospel Proclaimed
C: **Praise to you, O Christ.**

Sermon

Hymn: "Love, Love, Love" (Insert) (Herbert Brokering)

Our Response To God's Love

Offering And Announcements

Offertory

Confession Of Sin

L: Lord Jesus, we come before you confessing that we have not loved you with our whole hearts nor have we loved our neighbors as ourselves.

C: **Forgive us for withholding our love, All Caring God.**

L: Lord Jesus, we return to you all we have knowing that everything we are and possess are signs of your gracious love.

C: **Forgive us for boasting in ourselves and our possessions, Great Benefactor.**

L: For those times when we have spoken unkind words,

C: **Forgive us and do not hold them against us.**

L: For those things we have neglected to do for you and others,

C: **Forgive us and do not hold it against us.**

L: For our stubbornness in pursuing our own desires and not your will for our lives,

C: **Forgive us and deepen our commitment to you through Christ Jesus our Lord.**

Words Of Forgiveness Declared:

L: The God who created and loved you has heard your cries of repentance. Receive the forgiveness of your sins. In the name of the Father, the Son, and the Holy Spirit.

C: **Amen.**

Prayers From Renewed Hearts

L: Our hearts have been cleansed by the love of God poured out in Christ Jesus. Let us now offer our prayers unto God that his Spirit would work in our lives and situations. Let us pray.

Prayers Of The Church:

L: Lord, in your mercy,

C: Hear our prayer.

The Lord's Prayer

In Honor Of Mother's Day: A Thank You For Love — Insert *(Led by youth participants)*

A Thank You For Love

Y: As young people, blessed by God, to share that love with family and friends, we take time today to say "thanks" to all those women who make the lives of others special by their love and care.

C: We thank God and you for the gift of love.

Y: The Lord God made a companion for man and a mother for humankind. One side of God's love is seen for us in mothers.

C: We thank God for his creation and gift of love found in mothers.

Y: Women make houses more than structures that house bodies. Families need homes as places of refuge and love.

C: We thank mothers for filling our homes with their love and their presence.

Y: Memories of happy times bring smiles to our faces.

C: **We thank God and mothers for the gift of laughter and joy.**

Y: In times of sadness and disappointment, we are comforted by loving arms.

C: **We thank God for the shelter of a mother's understanding hug.**

Y: As a quilt wraps us up in the warmth of its cover,

C: **We thank God and mothers for the warmth of their love.**

Y: For the laundry, meals and cleaned up rooms,

C: **We thank you, tender caretakers.**

Y: For both the praise and corrections that come from your lips,

C: **Thank you, wise nurturers.**

All: **Mothers are God's gifts of love sent to us from heaven above. For that we give God thanks and praise. Amen.**

Benediction

Closing Hymn: "Love Divine, All Loves Excelling"

6

God's Shining Lights

Sunday Morning
Holy Communion

Call To Worship:

L: God has set us to be lights to the nations so that salvation would be known throughout all the earth. Let us praise the source of all light, Jesus Christ. As God's people, let us rise and shine as we declare the glory of God.

L: We call upon Christ to enter our presence as we worship.

C: Come, Holy Spirit, and quicken the flame of love in our hearts as we celebrate and praise Jesus, the True Light. Amen.

Hymn: "Rise, Shine, You People"

Litany Of Light

L: God spoke and there was light. And God saw that the light was good.

C: Creator God, fill us with your good light.

L: Source of goodness, as we turn toward you, let the light of your face shine upon us.

C: Glorious God, we behold your light.

L: Arise, shine; for your light has come;

C: And the glory of the Lord has risen upon us.

L: Those who lead many to righteousness will shine like stars forever and ever.

C: May we shine as stars with the brilliance of Jesus' life within.

L: Jesus is the light that shines in the darkness, but the darkness has not overcome it.

C: Holy Spirit, shine into our dark souls that we might understand Jesus.

L: Let your light shine before others.

C: May we reflect the glory of God. Amen.

The Light Reflected

Children's Choirs

The First Lesson

The Second Lesson

The Holy Gospel

Children's Message

A Message Of Light

Hymn: "Renew Me, O Eternal Light"

Offering And Announcements

Offertory: "Praise God From Whom All Blessings Flow"

Confession Of Darkness And Light

L: As we prepare to partake of the Lord's supper, we ask God to shine his light into our hearts and to reveal those areas of darkness.

C: **Search us, O God, and forgive us our sins.**

L: Once we were in darkness, but now in the Lord we are light.

C: **Forgive us, O God, for not living as children of light.**

L: For the fruit of the light is found in all that is good and right and true,

C: **Forgive us, O God, for not bearing good and proper fruit.**

L: God desires that we do what is pleasing in his sight.

C: **Forgive us our neglect of prayer and study, dear Lord.**

Absolution:

L: God's forgiveness is bestowed now in the name of the Father, the Son, and the Holy Spirit. Let his grace enable you to walk blameless and innocent, children without blemish in the midst of a crooked and perverse generation, so that you may shine like stars in the world.

C: We receive God's pardon and love. Amen.

Apostles' Creed

God's Light Revealed

L: As Christ prepared to share his last meal with his followers, he understood how darkness would soon overcome the world for a time. Yet his promise to them and to us comes in the light of his glorious resurrection. Hear his words and remember.

Words Of Institution

The Lord's Prayer

Distribution Of Communion

L: Let us pray: The Lord's body and blood strengthen and preserve you in his grace filling you with the light of his love.

C: Amen.

Recognizing Special Lights

L: Today we celebrate the last day of Sunday school and recognize the ministry of those who have shared their time, talent, and faith with our youth. We ask our Sunday school superintendent to come forward as we acknowledge those who have shared the light of Christ's love.

Recognition Of Teachers

Prayers Of The Church

L: Let us rise and pray: O God, we are so blessed to have been chosen to be your lights. Stir up your gifts within each of us that we may use them to your glory.

C: **We pray for your Spirit's anointing.**

L: For these special teachers and students in our congregation,

C: **We give you thanks and praise.**

L: For all those who seek to share your love in their specific areas of ministry,

C: **We ask for the outpouring of your Spirit.**

L: For those who are ill and in need of your healing touch, those who are grieving, those who are not able to be with us, especially ... (insert names)

C: **Bring health, and comfort, and your presence.**

L: All these prayers we bring to the light trusting in your divine and perfect will.

C: **Amen.**

Benediction

L: May the blessing of our immortal God go with us now. Trust in the Father's wisdom, lean on the Savior's strength, and flow with the Spirit's guidance. Go forth bringing God's light to the dark places. Shine with his love until the day dawns when the bright and morning star, Jesus Christ, will come once more and shine upon every heart.

C: **And the glory of the Lord go with us! Amen.**

Hymn: "Immortal, Invisible"

7

Litany Of Freedom

Memorial Day Observance

Introductory Comments:

(May or may not be printed on insert. If used, bulletin will be two-sided. If eliminated, bulletin will be one-sided.)

L: Since its establishment on May 30, 1868, Memorial Day has been a time set aside to remember those who have died in service to our nation. Wars and military conflicts have been a part of our nation's history and the world's problems. The Civil War, the World Wars, the Korean Conflict, Viet Nam and Desert Storm have all left their mark upon our nation.

Our Lord said in Matthew 24:6-8, "And you will hear of wars and rumors of wars; see that you are not alarmed; for this must take place, but the end is not yet. For nation will rise against nation, and kingdom against kingdom, and there will be famines and earthquakes in various places; all this is but the beginning of the birthpangs."

God does not cause wars to happen. Self-interest, greed, and other sins enter into the hearts of nations and rulers. The result is conflict. God is grieved when this happens. He mourns the loss of those who fall in battle. Let us now take time to remember those loved ones who have given their lives for the freedoms which we as a nation now enjoy.

Litany Of Freedom

L: Almighty God, we praise you for the freedom we know in this United States of America.

C: **Remember those who gave their lives that we might keep this freedom.**

L: Precious Lord, comfort all who grieve for those who died serving this country during armed conflicts.

C: **Remember those serving in the armed forces around the world who uphold that freedom.**

L: Great Redeemer, thank you for protecting our troops serving in dangerous war zones.

C: **Remember those still stationed in the territories of unrest.**

L: For your great love and sacrifice,

C: **We praise you Lord.**

L: For the comfort we find in the knowledge that you are in control of the world,

C: **We praise you Lord.**

L: For the end of the war and the reign of peace,

C: **We praise you Lord.**

L: For freedom's privilege and blessing,

C: **We praise you Lord.**

L: Let us pray. Jesus, thank you for the sacrifice you gave us in your death and resurrection purchasing for us true freedom from sin and death. Lord in your mercy,

C: **Hear our prayer.**

L: Be with our nation as we honor those who have died for its freedom. Lord in your mercy,

C: **Hear our prayer.**

L: Be with our president, the leaders of our government, those in charge of our military, and all who work to maintain peace in our world. Lord in your mercy,

C: **Hear our prayer.**

L: Give wisdom and discernment in all policy-making and enable those seeking peace to work together so harmony can come to a world in disorder. Lord in your mercy,

C: **Hear our prayer.**

L: Protect us and keep us in your care until you come again to restore us to everlasting peace.

C: **Amen. Come soon, Lord Jesus.**

8

Behold The Glory
Of The Lord

Nursing Home Service
With Holy Communion

Invocation:

L: We come together today to worship Jesus the King. Come, Holy Spirit, and fill us with your presence that we might glorify the Father in heaven. Breathe on us breath of God that we might offer true worship and praise. Behold, the glory of the Lord!

C: Come and let us worship King Jesus. Amen.

Hymn: "Oh, Worship The King"

God's Glory Acclaimed

L: The heavens declare the glory of God,

C: And the skies proclaim his handiwork.

53

L: Be exalted, O God, above the heavens,

C: And let your glory be all over the earth.

L: Ascribe to the Lord, O heavenly beings,

C: Ascribe to the Lord glory and strength.

L: Ascribe to the Lord the glory of his name,

C: Let us worship the Lord in holy splendor.

L: O Lord, our Sovereign God, how majestic is your name in all the earth;

C: You have set your glory above the heavens.

L: Blessed be God's glorious name forever;

C: May his glory fill the whole earth.

L: Lift up your heads, O worshipers of God;

C: We lift our heads and see the King of Glory!

L: Fling wide the gates of your hearts that the King of Glory may come in;

C: We open the doors of our hearts that the King of Glory may enter in.

L: Who is this King of Glory?

C: It is the Lord of Hosts, Christ Jesus. He is the King of Glory. Amen.

Prayer Of The Day

L: Let us pray: Almighty God, we hail you as our Lord and king. As the heavens and earth declare your majesty, we thank you that we can see your glory revealed to us in your Son, Jesus. As you glorified him by his death and resurrection, glorify us as we die to our old lives and are raised to new life in Christ Jesus. Amen.

The Word Reveals God's Glory

The First Lesson

The Second Lesson

The Gospel

Meditation On God's Glory

Hymn: "Blessing And Honor"

Jesus Reveals His Glory

L: We gather now as the body of Christ to give glory and praise to the Lamb by remembering Jesus' death and resurrection. Let us examine our hearts and confess our sin that we might come to the Lord's Table and receive his forgiveness and restoration.

C: **Wash us in the blood of the Lamb.**

L: For our many sins which separate us from you, Almighty God,

C: **Forgive and cleanse us, O Lamb of God.**

55

L: For the thoughts which we have had that are not pleasing in your sight,

C: **Forgive and cleanse us, blessed Holy Spirit.**

L: For the actions which we have not taken which we felt prompted to do,

C: **Give us another opportunity to serve.**

L: For those words we have spoken which have hurt others,

C: **Forgive us and restore us to others.**

L: For deeds which have harmed others,

C: **Forgive and bring healing.**

L: Help us to die to ourselves that we might reflect your glory, Gracious Lord.

C: **We offer ourselves and all we have up to you, Merciful God. Receive us through Jesus Christ our Savior and our Lord. Amen.**

Absolution

L: Having confessed our sin, hear God's words of grace: Receive pardon and forgiveness in the name of the Father, the Son, and the Holy Spirit.

C: **Amen.**

Celebration Of Holy Communion

L: Restored to God through Christ Jesus our Lord, we come and receive his precious body and blood. Hear the words of love spoken by our Lord and remember.

Words Of Institution

The Lord's Prayer

Our Father, who art in heaven, hallowed be thy name, thy kingdom come, thy will be done, on earth as it is in heaven. Give us this day our daily bread; and forgive us our trespasses, as we forgive those who trespass against us; and lead us not into temptation, but deliver us from evil. For thine is the kingdom, and the power and the glory, forever and ever. Amen.

Distribution Of Communion

Benediction

L: And now may the body and blood of our Lord Jesus Christ strengthen and preserve you. Go forth today glorifying your Father in heaven. Receive his blessing in the name of the Father, who loves you, the Son, who redeemed you, and the Holy Spirit, who empowers you.

C: Amen.

Hymn: "Joyful, Joyful We Adore Thee"

9
Healing Of Divisions

Prayer Service

Hymn: "What A Friend We Have In Jesus"

Call To Prayer:

L: Jesus, our dearest friend, calls us to humbly come into the very presence of our loving Father through this service of prayer. The Lord is giving us the privilege of standing in the gap as we pray in intercession for our hurting world. Society is fragmented, torn with the pain of divisions of all kinds. So we ask the Lord's healing on all as we pray.

C: **Take us into your presence, dear God, as we join our hearts in prayer. Amen.**

The Word Proclaims God's Presence:

L: God gives us his promise of power through prayer and his presence with us. Hear that promise from the Gospel of Matthew.

C: **Glory to you, O Lord.**

Gospel Reading: Matthew 18:18-20

L: The Gospel of the Lord.

C: **Praise to you, O Christ.**

God Calls His Children To Adore Him

L: The Lord calls us to recognize that we are his and all we have is his. Let us praise and adore the God who has blessed us.

Litany Of Praise Based On Psalm 8

L: O Lord, our Lord, how majestic is your name in all the earth!

C: **Almighty God, we praise your holy name.**

L: God's glory is seen in the heavens.

C: **Glorious Lord, we lift up our praise.**

L: Out of the mouths of babes and infants, you have ordained praise, because of your foes, to silence the enemy and the avenger.

C: **Victorious Lord, open our mouths to praise which defeats the enemy.**

L: When we look at the heavens, the work of God's fingers, the moon and the stars he has created; we ask what are human beings that he cares for us so?

C: **Creator God, we praise you for your loving care.**

L: Yet God made us a little lower than himself, and crowned us with glory and honor.

C: **King of Kings, we praise you for that honor.**

L: God has given us dominion over the works of his hands. He put all created things under that authority.

C: **For all you have made, we praise you, O God.**

L: O Lord, our Lord, how majestic is your name in all the earth!

C: **Great Majesty, we praise your holy name!**

Call To Confession And God's Absolution

L: The Word tells us that all have sinned and fall short of the glory of God. But God promises us that if we confess our sins, he will forgive us those sins through the blood of his Son, Jesus. Let us take a moment to examine our hearts in silence and to confess our sins before God so that we may approach the throne boldly in prayer.

Silence For Confession

L: As you have confessed your sins and been washed in the blood of Christ, receive forgiveness in the name of the Father, the Son, and the Holy Spirit.

C: **Amen.**

God Desires Justice For All

L: Injustice in our world pains the Father's heart and brings division. Hear from the Word what God requires to bring healing.

Reading: Micah 6:8

L: Let us pray: God of Justice, as you have shown grace to us, your children, prompt us to be merciful to others. We pray for justice for all people. We pray for the elimination of the underlying causes of injustice that tear societies apart. Bring healing to the hearts of the wounded. Fill us with compassion so we may understand and be instruments of love.

Congregational Petitions For Justice

L: Lord, in your mercy,

C: Hear our prayer.

God Loves All People

L: Today's society is torn apart in many ways, by racism, exploitation of others, greed, pride, and so much more. God desires his family, united in Christ, to be whole and healthy. Hear from the Word what God desires.

Reading: Galatians 3:26-28

L: Let us pray: Father of All, we pray for an end to racism in our nation and in the world. Help us to see all human beings as created in your image and to respect and honor them as you honor us. Put an end to the exploitation of others that all might share in your blessings through faith in Christ Jesus our Lord.

Congregational Petitions For The End To Prejudice

L: Lord, in your mercy,

C: Hear our prayer.

God Desires Us To Be One

L: Hate is a force which tears apart our oneness. Hear from the Word what God desires to bring healing.

Reading: 1 John 4:20-21

L: Let us pray: Loving God, you call us to be one in you through Christ Jesus our Lord. We pray that love will heal the pain and hate which rests in so many hearts. We pray for those who have lost loved ones and property as a result of the unrest, frustration, and anger that has taken root in those disenfranchised in our society. Let your healing flow.

Congregational Petitions For Unity And Oneness

L: Lord, in your mercy,

C: **Hear our prayer.**

Prayers For Our Nation And Government

L: Authority and power are in God's hands. In this world we live as a nation under God praying that our government will guide us wisely. Hear Jesus' words and his desire for us.

Reading: Matthew 28:18-20

L: Let us pray: King of kings, we pray for our nation and those who govern and lead us. Plant the gifts of integrity and honor in those who make and enforce our laws. Give voice to those who speak out for those with no power or voice. Grant wisdom to those empowered by law and common consent that they might be led by your Spirit. May we truly be a nation of God seeking his will and not our own. Grant that as a godly nation we may use our blessings to further his kingdom upon earth.

Congregational Petitions For Nation And Government

L: Lord, in your mercy,

C: **Hear our prayer.**

Prayers For Our Congregation

L: God calls us not to worry about worldly things but to be concerned about him and his kingdom here on earth. Hear from the Word what God desires and what brings healing.

Reading: Romans 12:1-2

L: Let us pray: Lord Jesus, look down with favor upon us, your congregation of believers. Pour out your Spirit as we seek your perfect will. Help us to set aside our unforgiveness, our judgment of others, and anything else that might separate us from you and others. Guide us to seek that which is good, pleasing, and needed for your perfect will to be accomplished in our lives and in the life of this congregation. Be at the center of our worship, our programs, our fellowship, our outreach — our lives. May we always walk in harmony with you and one another through Christ our Lord.

Congregational Petitions — Church And Individual

L: Lord, in your mercy,

C: Hear our prayer.

L: As we have lifted our petitions to a loving and merciful God, who has heard the prayers of our lips and knows those unspoken upon our hearts, be assured that God will answer according to his perfect will. And so we close with the prayer Christ taught us to pray.

The Lord's Prayer

Benediction

L: Go now in peace and continue to let God bring healing of all divisions. In the name of the Father who unites us, the Son who heals us, and the Spirit who empowers us.

C: Amen.

Hymn: "All Praise To Thee, My God."

64

10

A Celebration Of Baptism

Baptism
Worship Service

Introductory Comments

This service is designed to assist us as a congregation to enlarge and enhance the place Baptism holds in the faith and life of each of us as members of the body of Christ. The sacrament of Holy Baptism is not a simple water act, but water combined with God's command and Word make it a gift from the God of life as we are washed in the regeneration of the Holy Spirit. Therefore, we gather to affirm our faith in Christ and the waters into which we were buried and then raised to new life through belief in Jesus our Lord and Savior.

And so, we begin our worship in the name of the Father, the Son, and the Holy Spirit in whose name we were baptized.

The Word Speaks Of Baptism

L: Christ Jesus, our Lord, tells us in the last chapter of Matthew: "Go and teach all nations, baptizing them in the name of the Father and of the Son and of the Holy Spirit."

C: **We rejoice in our baptismal grace.**

L: Christ Jesus, our Lord, tells us in the last chapter of Mark: "Those who believe and are baptized, will be saved; but those who do not believe will be condemned."

C: **We rejoice in our baptismal grace.**

L: Paul tells us in the third chapter of Titus: "God saved us through the washing of rebirth and renewal by the Holy Spirit, whom he poured out on us generously through Jesus Christ our Savior, so that, having been justified by his grace, we might become heirs having the hope of eternal life. This is a trustworthy saying."

C: **We rejoice in our baptismal grace.**

L: Paul also tells us in the sixth chapter of Romans: "We were buried with Christ through baptism into death in order that, just as Christ was raised from the dead through the glory of the Father, we too may live a new life.

C: **We rejoice in our new life in Christ Jesus our Lord as we are united with him in his death and resurrection. Amen.**

Opening Hymn

First Lesson

Second Lesson

Gospel

Baptismal Message

Hymn

God Calls To Us Through Baptism

L: Jesus Christ came into the world to free it from sin and death, but the world did not recognize its Savior. His own people did not receive him, but to those who did believe in his name, he gave the right to become children of God. John the Baptist cried out to the people, "Repent and believe." John baptized with water but awaited the one who would baptize with fire, Jesus the Christ. Jesus Christ hung on the cross, yet the people would not believe. But when the good news of his death and resurrection was proclaimed, many believed and wanted to know what to do. Peter replied, "Repent and be baptized, every one of you, in the name of Jesus Christ for the forgiveness of your sins. And you will receive the gift of the Holy Spirit. The promise is for you and your children and for all who are far off — for all whom the Lord our God will call." Let us rise and declare our faith in God through our baptism. *(Congregation rises.)*

We Respond To God's Baptismal Grace

L: Do you hear God calling to you through the waters of your baptism?

C: **We hear the call to respond to our baptism.**

L: God gives us many opportunities to witness to our faith in Jesus Christ as Lord. One of those ways is to bear witness to the faith we profess by living in the covenant of our baptism and in communion with the church. I ask you now to profess your faith in Jesus as Lord and Savior, to reject sin, and to confess the faith of the church, the faith in which you were baptized.

67

L: Do you renounce all the forces of evil, the devil, and all his empty promises?

C: I do.

L: Do you believe in God the Father?

C: I believe in God, the Father Almighty, Creator of heaven and earth.

L: Do you believe in Jesus Christ, the Son of God?

C: I believe in Jesus Christ, his only Son, our Lord. He was conceived by the power of the Holy Spirit and born of the Virgin Mary. He suffered under Pontius Pilate, was crucified, died, and was buried. He descended into hell. On the third day he rose again. He ascended into heaven, and is seated at the right hand of the Father. He will come again to judge the living and the dead.

L: Do you believe in God the Holy Spirit?

C: I believe in the Holy Spirit, the Holy Catholic Church, the communion of saints, the forgiveness of sins, the resurrection of the body, and the life everlasting. Amen.

L: As God, the Father of our Lord and Savior Jesus Christ, poured out his Spirit upon him at his baptism, so he liberated us from the power of sin and raised us to new life through the sacrament of baptism. The Spirit was poured out at that time: the spirit of wisdom and understanding, the spirit of counsel and might, the spirit of knowledge and the fear of the Lord, the spirit of joy in God's presence.

C: Spirit of the Living God, fall afresh on us.

L: Through baptism, we were made brothers and sisters, members of the priesthood we all share in Christ Jesus our Lord. We proclaim the praise of our God as we bear his creative and redeeming Word to all the world.

C: **Spirit of the Living God, fall afresh on us.**

L: Baptized into the death and resurrection of our Lord, we go forth to proclaim his salvation to the world.

C: **Send us forth with your anointing, Holy Spirit. Amen.**

Hymn

Invitation To The Waters

L: As we come to the Lord's table and are renewed through the sacrament of Holy Communion, I invite you to come to the waters of baptism and reaffirm your communion with Christ and be renewed by dipping your hand into the waters and placing the water upon your forehead in the sign of the cross. You were marked with that cross at your baptism to remind you of whose you are. Join us as we celebrate once more that gift of grace given to us by God in Christ Jesus, the baptizer.

C: **We celebrate the gift of baptism.**

Opportunity To Reaffirm Baptism

(Those wishing to reaffirm their spiritual birthday are welcome to come forward at this time.)

Special Music

The Comfort Of Our Baptism

L: There is no greater comfort than the sacrament of baptism for it is God's gift to us in Christ Jesus. Therefore, we seek God's perfect will in our lives and in the lives of those we pray for. Lord, in your mercy,

C: **Hear our prayer.**

Prayers Of Intercession

L: We place these petitions, spoken and unspoken, before the throne of grace, praising our Lord who hears our cries and answers according to his most perfect will.

C: **Amen.**

The Lord's Prayer

Empowered To Witness

L: Go forth now, renewed and refreshed, through the worship of God in communion with Christ under the anointing of the Holy Spirit. Empowered to witness to your baptismal grace, be lights in a darkening world. Shine forth with the love and power we have in knowing that Jesus Christ truly is Lord. Amen.

Closing Hymn

Baptism —
A Birthday Celebration

Texts: Acts 22:6-16; Matthew 28:16-20

Grace and peace to you, my brothers and sisters. Today we celebrate at this special worship our Christian birthday — our baptismal day.

Baptism is a sacrament for us in the church. The word "sacrament" comes from the Latin word *sacramentum* which was the Roman soldier's oath of absolute devotion and obedience to his general.

Jesus has given us two special commands to follow — Communion (Matthew 26): He said, "Do this ..."; and in the gospel text for today (Matthew 28), his final instructions to his followers: "Go — baptize — teach." Note that Jesus does not simply say "be baptized." We are to "go" and to "teach" as well as to be baptized.

Mother Theresa of Calcutta is a modern example of one living out her baptism — going and teaching. There were times when this commitment made her unconverted neighbors furious. They shunned her at times and harassed her, even shouting after her as she made her way down the streets. "You're the ugliest woman I ever saw," one of them ridiculed her. Gently she turned this attack aside. "Isn't it wonderful how God can love an ugly, old woman like me!" she replied.

Baptism is God's great love reaching down to touch and to renew us giving us new life — a new life that leads to eternal life.

"All persons are created equal" is the basis for our democracy, but there has always been a question about what equality means. People are not equal in physical size or power. They surely are not equal in importance or in the value society places upon their work. Starting salaries for a school teacher and a professional baseball player are drastically different. Money and social standing are false measuring rods. Therefore, there is a need to recognize the true values in life: the fact that every human being is precious in God's sight.

Jesus dealt equally with all — rich, poor, employers, laborers, priests, kings, socialites, outcasts, prodigals, tax collectors, women, children, even a thief and a traitor. He gave his life for them all. As we die with Christ in the waters of baptism and receive new life, we are given a new name — Christian. We become one with Christ and celebrate one baptism, one family, one Lord. In Jesus we find the one hope of life which unites us as one — equals in the new life.

Pastors visiting with parents about to have a child baptized spend a good part of the time emphasizing the point that baptism — while complete — as a gift is only useful as it is utilized. Jesus expects us to use that gift. It is not a gift to receive and then to stuff away in some far corner of our lives. Martin Luther said that we need to come to the waters of our baptism daily. There is no point to having a new life if we keep living the old life.

Baptismal vows (those oaths we share as equals — brothers and sisters of the same family) point us in the direction of this new life we are to live. As sponsors present a candidate for baptism, they state that they will faithfully bring the baptized to the services of God's house. This means in our baptismal life that we are to faithfully gather for worship as a baptized community celebrating that gift of grace. A recent study disclosed that if both parents attend church regularly, 72 percent of their children remain faithful. It also showed that if only one partner attends regularly, 55 percent remain faithful. If only the mother attends regularly, 15 percent remain faithful. If neither parent attends regularly, only six percent remain faithful.

Sponsors also state that they will teach the baptized the Lord's Prayer, the Creed, and the 10 commandments. In order to teach another, one needs to know the subject. Even better than that we need to live by that which we seek to help others to learn and use as guides for their life.

Finally, of utmost importance, we are to place in the hands of the baptized the holy scriptures. The Bible is truly the best guide for living our new life. Other books may help us to better understand and to give us insight, but they can and should never replace our own reading of God's Word.

It is paramount that we live out our baptismal promise because baptism is not some sort of magical event that guarantees eternal life. In fact, Paul in Acts 22 makes this point: "Get up, be baptized, and have your sins washed away, calling on his (Jesus) name." It is the calling on Jesus' name, not the getting up or the being baptized, that brings the washing of sins. Luther said that there are many who act as if baptism gives them an indulgence to sin and the privilege of presuming on the grace of God. But this is decidedly not the purpose of baptism. He further speaks of baptism as a ship: "It carries all who are brought to the harbor of salvation: It is the truth of God giving us its promise in the sacrament. Of course, it does happen that many rashly leap from the ship into the sea and perish. These are they who depart from faith in the promise and plunge into sin. If any would return to the ship, God's grace is there to assist and once again they are borne on to life. This is he who returns to the stable and settled promise of God through faith."

Baptism is our ship of salvation, but we must stay on board. This means that by our faith we must cling tightly to the one in whose life we have been buried and reborn.

Happy Christian birthday! Your baptismal day. Amen.

11

A Galilean
Service

Lakeside Service
With Communion

(Based on Matthew 4:12-23)

L: Jesus began his public ministry in the area of Galilee to fulfill what the prophet Isaiah had said: "Land of Zebulun and land of Naphtali, the way to the sea, along the Jordan, Galilee of the Gentiles — the people living in darkness have seen a great light; on those living in the land of the shadow of death a light has dawned."

C: **As the sun begins to set and darkness begins to surround us, we remember that we walk in the light of Christ Jesus our Lord.**

L: John the Baptist stood at the waters of the Jordan calling the people to repent of sin.

C: **As we touch the waters of baptism through repentance, we are raised to new life through belief in Christ Jesus as Lord.**

L: Jesus walked by the Sea of Galilee and called Simon Peter and Andrew who were fishing to come and follow him.

C: **As we hear Christ's voice and respond, we, too, become fishers of those yet lost.**

L: Jesus went throughout Galilee, teaching, preaching, and healing.

C: **As we gather tonight in worship, Jesus stands in our midst to teach us more about God's will, to share with us more of God's plan for our lives, and to heal us in body, mind, and spirit through his mercy.**

L: Come, let us worship the Lord.

C: **We cry out, come Lord Jesus. Amen.**

Hymn: "On Jordan's Banks The Baptist's Cry"

Christ's Ministry To Those Around The Lake

(Based on Mark 6:14-52)

L: After the murder of John the Baptist, Christ withdrew by boat to a solitary place, but the crowds followed him on foot from the towns.

C: **Look upon us with compassion and mercy and heal us, O Lord.**

L: As evening approached, the crowds hungered.

C: **Look upon us with compassion and mercy and feed us, O Lord.**

L: Five thousand were fed from five loaves of bread and two fish.

C: **Look upon us with compassion and mercy and fill us, O Lord.**

L: Jesus then commanded his disciples to get into the boat and go ahead of him while he dismissed the crowd and went out to pray.

C: **Look upon us with compassion and mercy and pray for us, O Lord.**

L: Jesus came walking on the water as the winds and waves crashed around the disciples' boat.

C: **Look upon us with compassion and mercy and calm the storms of our lives, O Lord.**

L: Peter stepped out and walked to Jesus but began to sink when he took his eyes off the Lord and put them on the waves.

C: **Look upon us with compassion and mercy and keep our eyes fixed on you, O Lord.**

L: The wind died down as Christ entered the boat, and the disciples were amazed.

C: **Look upon us with compassion and mercy and enter the boats of our lives, O Lord.**

L: Those in the boat began to worship Jesus, saying, "Truly you are the Son of God."

C: **We look upon you, O Jesus Christ, and worship you, O Son of God. Amen.**

Hymn Of Praise: "All Praise To Thee"

The Word Ministers To Us

Psalm 42

Old Testament Lesson: Isaiah 9:1-7

Gospel Lesson: Luke 5:1-11

The Good News Proclaimed: Meditation

Hymn

We Respond To The Word

L: As we have received the Word of God in our heart, we respond in our witness confessing the faith of the church, the faith in which we baptize.

Apostles' Creed

L: Let us now pray for the whole people of God in Christ Jesus and for all people according to their needs.

Petitions Of The Community

L: Lord, in your mercy,

C: Hear our prayer.

L: Into your hands, O Lord, we commend all for whom we pray, trusting in your mercy; through your Son, Jesus Christ our Lord.

C: Amen.

L: As Christ took the loaves and fishes and multiplied them to feed the multitude, so we now take the opportunity to give unto him our offering of thanksgiving for this night.

Offering

Offertory Prayer

L: Receive our offering, Lord Jesus Christ, which we present unto you with grateful hearts.

C: **Amen.**

The Lord Feeds Us With His Presence

L: As Jesus fixed breakfast for his disciples by the sea following his resurrection and invited them to eat with him, so he now invites us to his table remembering him in holy communion and through the prayer he taught us to pray.

The Lord's Prayer

L: On the night he was betrayed, Jesus took bread, gave thanks, broke it and gave it to his disciples, saying, "Take and eat; this is my body, given for you. Do this in remembrance of me."

After supper, he took the cup, gave thanks, and gave it for all to drink, saying, "This cup is the new covenant in my blood, shed for you and for all people for the forgiveness of sin. Do this for the remembrance of me."

We sit with Christ as the disciples did that night in remembrance of what he did for us in reconciling us to the Father through his death and resurrection. We share in this communion service by the lake by taking the body and blood in remembrance of him.

Christ Feeds Us

Distribution Of Communion

Communion Hymns

Our Response Of Love

(Based on John 21:1-19)

L: Following his resurrection and the feeding of the disciples on the Galilean shore, Jesus looked to Peter and looks to us to respond to his act of love for us. He turns to us and asks, "My precious children, do you truly love me more than these?"

C: **Yes, Lord, you know we love you.**

L: "Feed my lambs." Again Jesus asks, "My precious children, do you truly love me?"

C: **Yes, Lord, you know that we love you.**

L: "Take care of my sheep." And a third time, Jesus asks us, "My precious children, do you love me?"

C: **We turn to you now declaring, "Lord, you know all things; you know that we love you."**

L: Jesus says, "Feed my sheep."

C: **As you have fed us, O Lord, and restored us to fellowship with you, may we grow in love toward you and toward one another. Amen.**

Benediction

L: To this response, may the Lord bless us and keep us, the Lord make his face shine upon us and be gracious unto us, the Lord look with favor upon us and give us peace. In the name of the Father, the Son, and the Holy Spirit.

C: **Amen.**

Closing Hymn: "Now The Day Is Over"

12

Showers Of
Blessing

Worship Service
With A Skit

Leader's Helps

"Showers Of Blessing" is a program resource for use within the congregation. It involves a worship leader and reader for the service. The skit, "Bring Out God's Umbrellas," involves a leader and five Umbrella Women (J, E, S, U, S). The umbrella women hold up an upside down sign with an umbrella on it with the letters corresponding. When each is finished, they stay in line. The signs will spell out JESUS.

The worship service incorporates hymns, a confession, Apostles' Creed, scripture readings, the skit, and Lord's Prayer.

This resource may be used at a variety of events within the life of the church and would be especially helpful to a women's organization. Its purpose is to encourage worship centered on Jesus.

Showers Of Blessing

Call To Worship

L: We come together to share in a day of fellowship, learning, and worship. Let us unite in heart and purpose to receive God's blessings and love.

C: **Be present in our day, O Lord. Amen.**

Opening Hymn: "There Shall Be Showers Of Blessing" by El Nathan and James McGranahan (insert)

The Individual Is Showered By Mercy

Confession

L: The Lord richly blesses those who call upon him.

C: **We call upon the Lord to be present.**

L: God promises that as we read his Word, and hear it, and take it to heart, we will be blessed.

C: **Forgive us for neglecting our study of scripture and not honoring your Word.**

L: Elijah prayed earnestly that it would not rain, and it did not rain for three and a half years. Again he prayed, and the heavens gave rain, and crops were produced.

C: **We have not because we do not ask. Increase our times of prayer and bring our wills in line with yours.**

L: Jesus stood in the temple and called the thirsty to come and drink living water.

82

C: **Quench our thirst with your Spirit, O Lord, and revive our parched souls.**

L: The Lord hears your confession and requests. With truly repentant hearts, receive his forgiveness through Jesus Christ our Lord.

C: **Pour out your mercy upon us, O God. Amen.**

The Community Is Showered With Purpose

L: As a community of believers united in Jesus Christ, we confess our faith through the Apostles' Creed.

The Apostles' Creed:

I believe in God, the Father Almighty, Creator of heaven and earth. I believe in Jesus Christ, his only Son, our Lord. He was conceived by the power of the Holy Spirit and born of the Virgin Mary. He suffered under Pontius Pilate, was crucified, died, and was buried. He descended into hell. On the third day he rose again. He ascended into heaven, and is seated at the right hand of the Father. He will come again to judge the living and the dead. I believe in the Holy Spirit, the Holy Catholic Church, the communion of Saints, the forgiveness of sins, the resurrection of the body, and the life everlasting. Amen.

The Lord Showers Blessings

Old Testament Reading: Ezekiel 34:11, 25-31

Gospel Reading: John 12:12-13

L: Jesus, our Good Shepherd, cares for us and asks us to care for others in his name.

C: Hosanna! Blessed are those who come in the name of the Lord!

Bring Out God's Umbrellas — A skit

Blessed To Be A Blessing

Hymn: "Make Me A Blessing" by George Schuler (insert)

L: Blessed by God to be blessings, let us rise and pray the prayer Jesus taught us to pray receiving his blessing in our community so that we may share that blessing with others.

C: Our Father, who art in heaven, hallowed be thy name, thy kingdom come, thy will be done, on earth as it is in heaven. Give us this day our daily bread, and forgive us our trespasses, as we forgive those who trespass against us; and lead us not into temptation, but deliver us from evil. For thine is the kingdom, and the power, and the glory, forever and ever. Amen.

Doxology Sung: "Praise God From Whom All Blessings Flow"

Bring Out God's Umbrellas

L: Umbrellas have been around for a long time. We see them today as indispensable in warding off rain. But 200 years ago, when they were first introduced in England by a great humanitarian, Jonas Hanway, they were ridiculed. Hanway's travels in foreign countries had brought him in contact with the umbrellas. He felt they would be readily accepted in his land. So for 30 years, Hanway carried his umbrella. But young boys pelted him with cabbages and rotten eggs considering him "peculiar." He became known as the "umbrella man." But eventually people stopped poking fun at him as they recognized the umbrella's usefulness. Today few people would be without one.

Today we would like to turn the umbrella around — making it an object, not to ward off showers, but one which receives the showers of God's blessing. In order to do this, we need to introduce you to five Umbrella Ladies. First we have a representative from Luke 8:1-3:

"Soon afterwards he went on through cities and villages, proclaiming and bringing the good news of the kingdom of God. The 12 were with him, as well as some women who had been cured of evil spirits and infirmities: Mary, called Magdalene, from whom seven demons had gone out, and Joanna, the wife of Herod's steward, Chuza, and Susanna, and many others, who provided for them out of their resources."

J Woman: *(Holds up umbrella sign w/script on back.)* I represent all the faithful women in the Bible. Like Mary, JOANNA, Susanna, and all the others who cared for JESUS in their ministry, I witness JESUS in all I do. I call to you to witness the good news by going forth in JOY. Let the JOY of your salvation be proclaimed by your words and actions in order to promote healing and wholeness in the church, our society, and the world.

L: Women centered on JESUS can be powerful witnesses by their example. Let's meet another chosen by God and obedient to his call as found in Esther 5:1-2:

"On the third day Esther put on her royal robes and stood in the inner court of the king's palace, opposite the king's hall. The king was sitting on his royal throne inside the palace opposite the entrance to the palace. As soon as the king saw Queen Esther standing in the court, she won his favor and he held out to her the golden scepter that was in his hand. Then Esther approached and touched the top of the scepter."

E Woman: *(Holds up sign while reading.)* I, ESTHER, Queen by God's appointment to King Xerxes, who ruled over 127 provinces stretching from India to Cush, risked death that day. Approaching the king without being summoned might result in death unless the scepter was extended. But I was obedient to the call of God to step forward and speak for my people. God put me and puts you in positions to speak to and for others. We are all called and EMPOWERED by the Holy Spirit to witness to and EVANGELIZE those God puts in our sphere of influence. Let us ENTHUSIASTICALLY share with others and be ESTHERS all.

L: Women centered on JESUS, EAGER to ENTHUSIASTICALLY EVANGELIZE and share the knowledge of ETERNAL life, are a powerful force in the kingdom. But let us continue bringing forth some more women and introduce some loving SERVANTS from Luke 10:38-41:

"Now as they went on their way, he entered a certain village, where a woman named Martha welcomed him into her home. She had a sister named Mary, who sat at the Lord's feet and listened to what he was saying. But Martha was distracted by her many tasks; so she came to him and asked, 'Lord, do you not care that my sister has left me to do all the work by myself? Tell her then to help me.' But the Lord answered her, 'Martha, Martha, you are worried and distracted by many things; there is need of only one thing. Mary has chosen the better part, which will not be taken away from her.' "

S Woman: *(Holds up sign while reading.)* I represent the loving SERVANTS found throughout our church — women with differing gifts who work in cooperation with each other. SITTING at the feet of Jesus, we learn from him what he desires for our lives, and then we SET out to SERVE him in response to his love. Listening and listing our opportunities to SERVE enables each of us to grow in faith and affirm our own gifts and other's.

L: Women centered on JESUS, EAGER to ENTHUSIASTI-CALLY EVANGELIZE and share the knowledge of ETER-NAL life, being loving SERVANTS, show God's power in their lives. Let us hear of our next carrier of good news from Luke 23:55—24:1-3:

"The women who had come with Jesus from Galilee fol-lowed, and they saw the tomb and how his body was laid. Then they returned, and prepared spices and ointments. On the sab-bath they rested according to the commandment. But on the first day of the week, at early dawn, they came to the tomb, taking the spices that they had prepared. They found the stone rolled away from the tomb, but when they went in, they did not find the body."

U Woman: *(Holds up sign while reading.)* I am the caring com-munity of Christian women who are created in the image of God. I represent all of you who are called to discipleship in Jesus Christ. Centered on Christ and his plan for our lives, we are prepared to go and do what he commands. Like the women from Luke who cared for Christ's body after his death, God has called US all to be caretakers of his body, the church. As we seek to minister to others and share God's love, we come to an UNDERSTANDING of what discipleship is all about. The women at the tomb were prepared, and God calls US to be prepared committing ourselves in service to Jesus as Lord and creating caring, UNDERSTANDING, Christian commu-nities wherever we go.

L: Women centered on JESUS, EAGER to ENTHUSIASTI-CALLY EVANGELIZE and share the knowledge of ETER-NAL life, being loving SERVANTS, creating caring, Christian communities filled with UNDERSTANDING and commit-ment, release the power of God's love into the world. Let us now hear from our final representative from Luke 2:36-38:

"There was also a prophet, Anna the daughter of Phanuel, of the tribe of Asher. She was of great age, having lived with her husband seven years after her marriage, then as a widow to the age of 84. She never left the temple but worshiped there with fasting and prayer night and day. At that moment she came, and began to praise God and to speak about the child to all who were looking for the redemption of Jerusalem.''

S Woman: *(Holds up sign while reading.)* I am Anna. What a privilege was given to me to behold my SAVIOR before I died. I represent all adoring SEEKERS. Waiting is hard for us all. I challenge each of you to wait as I did, disciplining yourself, and engaging in the ministry of prayer. As we do, we will recognize the SAVIOR in our midst. SEEING Jesus in others we will then reach out to SUPPORT one another in our callings. Become Annas, SINCERELY SEEK the SAVIOR in all you do. Then your eyes will behold the kingdom of God in your midst.

L: Women centered on JESUS, EAGER to ENTHUSIASTICALLY EVANGELIZE and share the knowledge of ETERNAL life, being loving SERVANTS, creating caring, Christian communities filled with UNDERSTANDING and commitment, adoring and SINCERELY SEEKING their SAVIOR, truly witness the power of God in their lives.

And so, we bring out God's umbrellas tipped to receive his blessings. Our church is a structure through which Jesus can move. You are the witnesses who bring life to that structure. Let your spirits be united in Christ's love bringing Jesus to those around you. As God has blessed you, go forth to bless others in Jesus' name. Amen.

13
Blessing Through Marriage

Anniversary Of Marriage Service

Hymn: "Blest Be The Tie That Binds"

Pastor: Jesus celebrated marriage at the wedding feast of Cana. Men and women for centuries have been blessed through this union of two in one. The writer of Ecclesiastes tells us that "Two are better than one, because they have a good reward for their toil. For if they fall, one will lift up the other; but woe to the one who is alone and falls and does not have another to help. Again, if two lie together, they keep warm; but how can one keep warm alone? And though one might prevail against another, two will withstand one. A threefold cord is not quickly broken."

The blessing of marriage is that we are united to another to walk this life by faith. With Christ as our third party, all things are possible. We remember today that bond recognized in marriage between _____ (name) and _____ (name) on _____ (date of wedding) as they celebrate their _____ (number of years together) anniversary. We

89

celebrate the word proclaimed in love and recall the blessing of that special day they were wed. Hear from 1 Corinthians 13 concerning love.

Reading: 1 Corinthians 13:1-13

Pastor: The gift of love is a blessing. This passage is often read at wedding ceremonies along with the passage on love from Ruth. Ruth here declares her love for her mother-in-law, a love that goes beyond the physical, and a love which we all desire to incorporate in our lives.

Reading: Ruth 1:16-17

Special Music

Pastor: Let us rise. As we celebrate the anniversary of _____ (name), let us pray to the God of love who has blessed us with their union. Let us pray:

> Loving God, you have blessed men and women for centuries in marriage. Your grace poured out for the daily living of our marriage vows has helped us in the rough times. Your joy infused into our spirits has enabled us to touch each other and our families in many special ways. For this we give you thanks.

Today we are especially thankful for the lives of _____ (name) and _____ (name). Continue to bless them as they celebrate their _____ (year) anniversary of marriage. Incline their hearts to be tender toward one another. Give them understanding and patience as they continue their journey through life. Encourage them to be faithful companions who desire to walk only with each other and hand in hand with you. Grant them health and strength in the days ahead. Be their companion and guide. Fill them with your love and increase that love they share for each other until they sit with you in heaven and celebrate the final marriage feast on high. Through Jesus Christ our Lord, we pray,

C: Amen.

Prayers For The Couple And Family

(Those assembled may be invited to offer petitions and thanks-givings. Prayers conclude with the Lord's Prayer.)

The Lord's Prayer

Blessing Benediction

Pastor: May Jesus Christ who has blessed us in this life, continue to bring joy to our marriages and to us as his children. Women, may you present yourselves before your bridegroom, Jesus Christ, pure and spotless in your wedding gown of faith. Men, may you honor your brides as Christ honors the church. And may the blessing of the Lord be upon us as we go forth celebrating life and Christ Jesus our Lord.

C: Amen.

Hymn: "Joyful, Joyful, We Adore Thee"

14
The Blessing
Of Giving
Post-Lenten
Ingathering Service

L: Brothers and sisters in Christ, as we have completed our Lenten journey and celebrated the death and resurrection of our Lord Jesus Christ, we have become aware of the many blessings in our lives. God has blessed us as members of the family of Christ in so many ways, but above all we realize the blessing of Jesus, God's Son, the most precious gift we have ever received. Christ has risen to conquer death and bestow upon us the gift of salvation. As a body of Christ this Lent we journeyed setting aside monies for specific ministry outreach in our congregation. The offerings that each of you have daily given will now be collected and offered to God to multiply and use to further the work of his kingdom through our church. Let us hear what the Word has to say concerning our offerings.

Reading: from Malachi 3:10-12

L: As we give unto the Lord, he will rain down showers of blessing. The prophet Ezekiel reminds us of this as he states that God will bless his people and their lambs sending down showers in season. There will be "showers of blessing" for God's faithful and giving people (Ezekiel 34:26). As you have been blessed to be a blessing, you have given to God. We now receive your offerings in this time.

(Offerings brought forward while a hymn is played or sung.)

L: Having brought up our gifts, let us now rise and pray asking God's blessing upon them. Let us pray:

All: Most Gracious God, we thank you for our Lenten journey and the blessing we have received as we have studied your Word and taken time in prayer. Receive our offerings given from grateful hearts that others may know the truth of your love and grace. As we have been blessed by you, take these gifts so others may be blessed. Amen.

15

A Feast Of Worship

Following Soup And Sandwich Supper

We Prepare Our Hearts

L: Before we make soup, we have to be sure to make certain preparations. Ingredients have to be purchased. Pots have to be dug out. Willing hands have to come together to work in cooperation. And so it is with worship. There is a time of preparation that needs to occur which enables us to enter God's presence, to sit at his feet, to gaze upon Jesus, to open ourselves up to the Spirit that we might worship God in the right spirit. Let us take a few moments of silence now to prepare our hearts before entering the very presence of God.

Silence To Prepare For Worship

We Examine The Kettle

L: We would never think of putting our ingredients into a dirty kettle to cook. Our pot needs to be clean so what we brew in it will be edible. So it is with our hearts. We need a time of examination, a time to look closely at our relationship with God, a time to confess our sin, and then a time to have the dirt of our lives washed away by the blood of Christ as we are restored to God in love. Let us pause now and examine our hearts.

Silence For Examination and Confession

Cleaning The Pot

L: Let us rise and stand before the Lord: Lord, Jesus, we come before you knowing that you know us better than we know ourselves.

C: Have mercy on us, All Knowing God.

L: We confess unto you that we have not always been faithful to you.

C: Have mercy on us, O Faithful God.

L: We ask your forgiveness for those times we have failed to walk in your ways.

C: Have mercy on us, O Merciful God.

L: We acknowledge that there have been times when we have spoken words that have hurt you and others.

C: Have mercy on us, O Loving God.

L: We ask you to forgive us. Wash us in love and present us spotless before the Father as clean vessels for his work.

C: Cleanse us thoroughly, Holy Spirit. Amen.

Absolution

L: Almighty God has heard our cries and knows the condition of our spirits. Through Jesus Christ he cleanses us from all sin and enables us to be pure and holy in God's eyes. Receive the forgiveness of that sin and be restored to fellowship with the Father once more.

C: Amen.

We Praise The Cook

L: The Lord, our God, is the master chef of our lives. Our lives need to be yielded to the Spirit who stirs up our faith. God is to be praised as we bless him. He has prepared a feast for us and invites us to taste and see that it is good. Let us bless the Lord.

Litany Of Praise

(Based on Psalm 34)

L: I will bless the Lord at all times; his praise shall continually be in my mouth.

C: Open my mouth to praise you, O God.

L: My soul makes its boast in the Lord; let the humble hear and be glad.

C: Open my ears to hear you, O God.

L: O magnify the Lord with me, and let us exalt his name together.

C: Open my eyes to see you, O God.

L: I sought the Lord, and he answered me, and delivered me from all my fears.

C: **Open my mind to deliverance, O God.**

L: Look to him, and be radiant; so your faces shall never be ashamed.

C: **May my face radiate Christ's love, O God.**

L: This poor soul cried, and was heard by the Lord, and was saved from every trouble.

C: **May my troubles be wiped away like tears, O God.**

L: The angel of the Lord encamps around those who fear him, and delivers them.

C: **May your angels stand guard over my life, O God.**

L: O taste and see that the Lord is good; happy are those who take refuge in him.

C: **Fill my mouth with all your blessings, O God, that I may be filled with all good things. Amen.**

Listen To The Recipe

First Lesson: Genesis 27:1-10

Second Lesson: Matthew 22:1-14

Add The Ingredients

Meditation

L: God is constantly adding ingredients to our life of faith and creating a wonderful mixture of faith, hope, and trust in Jesus. There are times when we feel he turns up the heat as circumstances bring faith to a boil. There are times when faith seems cold as we walk away from God taking things in our own hands like Jacob. Then there are times when faith just simmers there: times when God adds, and we accept and let him stir us to new understandings. Prayer enables us to keep a constant temperature and proper balance in life. And so we close our service now, lifting up our prayers to God who sifts them through his perfect will. Let us pray:

Prayers Of Community

The Lord's Prayer

Benediction

Closing Hymn

16

A Dedication Of Hand Chimes

Dedication Of Gift
In Memorial

These hand chimes are being presented as a gift to *(name of church)* in memory of *(name)* by *(family/friends)* that God would be glorified in worship through them.

L: The psalmist tells us to sing and make music to the Lord as a part of our worship. We call upon God's Spirit now to be present as we dedicate these instruments of praise.

C: **O God, accept our praise in dedicating these tone chimes to your glory.**

L: As a congregation celebrating its worship of the Lord Jesus Christ, we recognize the life of *(insert name)* who is memorialized by the use of these tone chimes.

C: **With grateful hearts we accept this gift.**

L: As God inspires his servants to use the gifts he has blessed them with, so inspire those who will play these tone chimes.

C: **With hearts atuned to your Spirit, stir up your gifts in those who use these instruments.**

L: As our children, youth, and adults find more meaningful expressions of service and faith through the use of these tone chimes, expand their vision of ministry and make them one with these tone chimes, each other, and you.

C: **United through Christ, may he be reflected in the musical praises created by each player.**

L: As David used his harp to soothe King Saul, soothe our hearts through the music created by these tone chimes.

C: **Minister to our spirits through the graceful notes of these tone chimes.**

Prayer Of Dedication

L: Harmonious God, you have blessed your people with the ability to praise and worship you through music. Accept the gift of these tone chimes that we dedicate to your glory today. May the use of them in our worship be a blessing to all who play them and hear the music created by them. May hearts be lifted that are heavy. May spirits rejoice drawing closer to you through praise. May we be inspired not just for today but in the years to come through the use of this gift. We give you thanks and praise as we consecrate the gift to your holy services. Through Christ Jesus we pray.

C: **Amen.**

17
Installation Of Pastor

Receiving A New Leader

We Prepare For Worship

(Name of Presider)

Prelude

Announcements

Processional Hymn

Invocation:

L: We call upon the Lord to be present through his Holy Spirit as we gather in celebration uniting our hearts in one accord with the call of Christ upon this pastor and this congregation. Send forth your Spirit, Almighty God, as we worship you through this installation service. May your blessings be poured out upon the ministry of your faithful servants who seek to do your perfect will.

C: Amen. Come Holy Spirit.

The Word Stands Among Us

L: Scripture tells us that when two or three are gathered in Christ's name, he is present. Jesus is the Word of God made flesh and revealed to our hearts through the Spirit. Let us hear what the Spirit has to say to us through the reading of the written Word.

First Lesson

Anthem

Second Lesson

The Alleluia Verse

The Gospel

Meditation

The Hymn Of The Day

Service of Installation

(Name of Installing Minister)

L: Let us rise in prayer.

Prayer: Blessed Heavenly Father, we gather today to install one you have called to serve this congregation. We ask that your Spirit continue its work as you join the gifts of this pastor and those in this congregation. Help them to work in harmony with your will serving you in the church and community bearing witness to the love of Christ.

C: Amen. Unite us Holy Spirit.

L: We are all called to discipleship in Jesus Christ our Lord. Living out that call, we are joined to one another in faith. Let us confess that faith in the words of the Apostles' Creed.

C: **I believe in God, the Father Almighty, Creator of heaven and earth.**

I believe in Jesus Christ, his only Son, our Lord. He was conceived by the power of the Spirit and born of the Virgin Mary. He suffered under Pontius Pilate, was crucified, died, and was buried. He descended into hell. On the third day he rose again. He ascended into heaven, and is seated at the right hand of the Father. He will come to judge the living and the dead.

I believe in the Holy Spirit, the Holy Catholic Church, the communion of saints, the forgiveness of sins, the resurrection of the body, and the life everlasting. Amen.

(Congregation may be seated,)

L: As presiding official at this installation service, it is my privilege to act on behalf of the church to ask for the certification of call for this pastor.

Representatives of Church Elder/Council: As representatives of this congregation, who after prayerful deliberation did elect *(name of pastor)* to be our minister, we present him now for installation.

L: *(Name of pastor),* you have been called by this congregation to serve as their pastor. Hear what the Word has to say:

Reader 1: John 20:21-23

L: And again:

Reader 2: Matthew 28:18-20

L: Hear the words addressed to Timothy:

Reader 3: 1 Timothy 4:12-16

L: *(Name of pastor)*, in the presence of this congregation will you commit yourself to assuming this new responsibility now entrusted to you, and promise to discharge your duties in harmony with the governing constitutions of the church?

P: Yes, and I ask God to help me.

L: Will you preach and teach in accordance with the Holy Scriptures and the confessions of our national church body?

P: Yes, and I ask God to help me.

L: Will you share love, willingly serve, and faithfully pray for God's people? Will you nourish them by the Word and sacraments, and lead them by your own example in exercising the means of grace through faithful service and holy living?

P: Yes, and I ask God to help me.

L: Will you witness to your faith in the world, so that others may know of God's love because of what you say and do?

P: Yes, and I ask God to help me.

L: May God, who has planted in you the desire and will to do these things, graciously bestow strength and compassion upon you to carry these out through the power of the Holy Spirit.

C: Amen.

Congregational Response

L: As God's people, will you receive this messenger of Christ who stands before you as one sent by God to serve God's people and to share with them the message of salvation and the gospel of hope?

C: We will.

L: As a sign of your support and encouragement to his ministry, will you pray for him, give help and respect to him for his work's sake, and seek to live together in peace and harmony through unity with Christ Jesus as Lord?

C: We will.

L: *(Name of pastor),* the office of pastor of *(name of congregation)* is now committed to you in the name of the Father, and of the Son, and of the Holy Spirit.

C: Amen.

(Pastor kneels for the blessing.)

L: May Almighty God who raised the Lord Jesus from the dead, bestow upon this his faithful servant the power to boldly proclaim the good news of Christ's death and resurrection. May you be equipped daily with the promise of the Holy Spirit so that in his power you may be true and faithful to God in this calling. This we pray in the name of the Father, and of the Son and of the Holy Spirit.

C: Amen.

L: The Lord be with you.

C: And also with you.

(The peace of Christ is shared.)

God Hears And Answers Prayers

(Name of Installed Pastor)

L: As God has heard our prayers and answered them by calling us to share in his ministry here at *(name of church)*, so he continues to hear and answer the prayers of our hearts. Let us join now in offering our prayers of thanksgiving and intercession unto the Father in Heaven.

Prayers Of The Church

L: ... Lord, in your mercy,

C: Hear our prayer.

L: Into your hands, Almighty God, we entrust all for whom we pray, trusting in your mercy through Christ Jesus our Lord.

C: Amen.

The Lord's Prayer

Benediction

Recessional Hymn

18
For All The Saints

For All Saints' Day

Call To Worship

L: Almighty God, we gather in worship today honoring the saints of the church, those who have died believing in Christ this past year. Come now, with the host of heaven and all the saints who sing your unending praise, as we worship you in celebration.

Confession

L: We enter the temple to worship the Lord;

C: **We come before the throne of grace joining the saints of old, one in Christ our Lord.**

L: We understand that we cannot enter the Lord's presence through our own strength or merit, and so we stand before the Lamb of God and acknowledge our sinful ways.

C: We confess our sins, O Lord.

L: For those times when we have pursued our own interests instead of your perfect will for our lives.

C: We confess our sins, O Lord.

L: For those times when we have neglected to commune with you through prayer and study,

C: We confess our sins, O Lord.

L: For those moments we have not shared with those closest to us because of our busyness,

C: We confess our sins, O Lord.

L: For those times we have neglected the cries of the needy,

C: We confess our sins, O Lord.

L: For the times we have not treated our brothers and sisters in Christ with the love you have shown all peoples,

C: We confess our sins, O Lord.

Absolution

L: God our Creator absolves us of our sin through the precious blood of Jesus Christ our Lord. Receive the forgiveness of your sins allowing God to purge your hearts of all unrighteousness through the power of the Holy Spirit. Enter now the gates of worship with rejoicing, and join your voices with the Saints in praise.

Opening Hymn

Prayer Of The Day

L: Almighty God, your people are knit together into one body through Jesus Christ the Lord. Grant that we may work together in harmony as we model the lives of your faithful saints of the past. Help us to commit ourselves to showing the joy that we find in our salvation. Prepare us in love that we may witness your love to a hurting world. We pray through your Son, who lives and reigns with you on high and who has promised to come to take us home again.

C: Amen.

Anthem

First Lesson

Second Lesson

Gospel

Sermon

Hymn

Creed

L: Do you believe in God, the Creator?

C: I believe in God, the Father Almighty, Creator of heaven and earth.

I believe that God creates us his saints.

L: Do you believe in Jesus Christ?

C: I believe in Jesus Christ, his only Son, our Lord. He was conceived by the power of the Holy Spirit and born of the

Virgin Mary. He suffered under Pontius Pilate, was crucified, died, and was buried. He descended into hell. On the
third day he rose again. He ascended into heaven, and is
seated at the right hand of the Father. He will come again
to judge the living and the dead.

**I believe Christ will come to take all his saints home for their
eternal rest!**

L: Do you believe in the Holy Spirit?

C: **I believe in the Holy Spirit, the Holy Catholic Church, the
communion of saints, the forgiveness of sins, the resurrection of the body, and the life everlasting.**

I believe God empowers his saints to do his work on earth!

Offering And Announcements

Offertory

Litany Of Mercy

L: The grace of our Lord Jesus, the love of God, and the communion of the Holy Spirit be with you all.

C: **And also with you.**

L: In peace let us pray to the Lord on high,

C: **Lord, have mercy.**

L: For equality in justice and peace among the nations of the
world, let us pray to the Lord,

C: **Lord, have mercy.**

L: For those living in poverty, hunger, and homelessness, let us pray to the Lord,

C: **Lord, have mercy.**

L: For fresh vision for the ministry of our church to enable it to be a faithful witness in this community and the world, let us pray to the Lord,

C: **Lord, have mercy.**

L: For the daily ministries we each perform as called by your Spirit, let us pray to the Lord,

C: **Lord, have mercy,**

L: For our home, work, and church environments where we labor and love, let us pray to the Lord,

C: **Lord, have mercy.**

L: For all the saints who stand now before you and for those they have left who mourn, let us pray to the Lord,

C: **Lord, have mercy.**

L: For those who have died in our congregational family this year *(names)*, let us pray to the Lord,

C: **Lord, have mercy.**

L: Help, save, comfort, and defend us Merciful God that we may stand without blemish on the day you call us home.

C: **Come soon, Lord Jesus. Amen.**

The Lord's Prayer

Benediction

Closing Hymn